From AirBNB Guest
Julie O'Brien

D1708759

Air Be &

Me

AIR BE & ME – How being an Airbnb host can reaffirm our faith in the essential goodness of humanity and bring the world to our doors.

Copyright © 2018 by Trudy Ohnsorg

All rights reserved. Printed in the United States of America. No part of this book may be used or reproduced in any manner whatsoever without written permission except in the case of brief quotations embodied in critical articles or reviews.

This book is based upon the author's experiences as well as her interviews with Airbnb hosts and guests. Unless specifically authorized, last names and identifying information have been omitted to protect privacy.

Airbnb® is a trademark of Airbnb, Inc.

Published in Saint Paul, Minnesota by Bohemian Treehouse Press, LLC. For information, contact:

Bohemian Treehouse Press
1125 Burns Avenue - Carriage House
Saint Paul, MN 55106
info@AirBeNMe.com

Cover design by JAAD Book Design. Inside design by JAAD Book Design and Trudy Ohnsorg.

Photos by Trudy Ohnsorg unless otherwise indicated.

2nd edition

ISBN-10: 0-9996673-1-9

ISBN-13: 978-0-9996673-1-6

Air Be &

Trudy Ohnsorg

Me

How being an Airbnb host can reaffirm our faith in the essential goodness of humanity and bring the world to our doors.

Acknowledgements

A book is never the solitary work of a lone writer. So many people have contributed to the development of this work it will be difficult to list them all. However, at the risk of forgetting someone, I will try to especially thank the following people:

- The Airbnb hosts whose stories appear in this book and all the members of the Twin Cities Airbnb Host Club: you are inspiring.

- Deb Jacobsen and the Women of Words writing group: you led me to believe that this book was possible in the first place, helped me understand the mysterious world of publishing, and offered insight and wisdom at every step along the way.

- Nick Powley, Deborah Yungner, and the CoCreateX organization: you introduced me to countless resources and people, encouraged me along the way, and have been extraordinary neighbors.

- Lori Myren-Manbeck: I am delighted to collaborate with you and Inclusivi-Tee!

- Julia Burman, Tess Galati, Tom Linton, Shirley Spraguer, and Shelia Cunningham McComb: many thanks for your critical (but supportive) editing.

- And finally, Airbnb hosts around the world: you provided my first introduction to this amazing way to travel. You opened my eyes to experiences and insights I would never have gained otherwise, and did so with generosity and kindness. I would not have had the courage to try hosting, let alone write this book, if it hadn't been for you.

Thank you!

iv

Dedication

This book is for all of us, hosts and travelers, who have overcome our fear of the unknown to share a space with a stranger. There is truly nothing like this experience! Once you've tried it, it's hard to go back to "regular" traveling in impersonal hotels. Some of us never do.

Especially, this book is for my wonderful, amazing, fantastic guests who have blessed me with their generosity, their wisdom, and their creativity.

I am so grateful to you, my dear guests, for all that you have given me: conversations over coffee at the patio table on cool summer mornings; and spontaneous hugs and offers to host me at your own homes, all over the world. Not to mention the occasional gifts of soaps, chocolate, wine, and really good baked goods!

And last but not least, I am grateful for your artwork - delightfully left for me to find on the chalkboard in the kitchen, sketched into the guest book, or sent to me as a gift days after we said "goodbye."

I'm so happy we connected. This book is for you.

R Hi Trudy! I'm interested in reading your book. Can you tell me more about it?

-Reader

T Hi Reader - thanks for your interest! This is a book full of stories from Airbnb hosts and guests about the magic that happens when people share a space. - Trudy

R Hmmm.... Can you tell me more? Where are you located?

T Most of the stories take place in the Twin Cities. That is, Saint Paul and Minneapolis, Minnesota. There's also one from Western Wisconsin, but that's practically a suburb.

R What did you mean by "magic?"

T For many people, sharing a space transforms an ordinary visit into something special and memorable. You see the place through the eyes of a local. You have experiences that you would never have learned about otherwise. Sometimes, you form bonds of friendship with your host that can last for years after your stay is over. That is magic.

R Sure beats a hotel. I'm in!

T Wonderful! I'm guessing that you will have Airbnb stories of your own to share someday. Send them my way - I'd love to read them!

Contents

The author's back yard in April

Introduction

Trudy, Host of "Little Purple House (Dog Friendly)" www.airbnb.com/rooms/6300661

IT ALL STARTED SOMETIME IN THE SPRING OF 2015. I was considering leaving my very stable government job with the benefits and regular paycheck to join a consulting group working primarily with non-profits. I asked myself: "Just how am I going to make this work, financially?" I also asked other things like: "Are you insane, Trudy?" This was closely followed by: "You might starve, girl." And then I thought: "You could lose your house."

That's when it hit me: I could use my house. My adorable house could help me fund this grand adventure. I had stayed in Airbnbs during vacations for a couple of years. I spent one delightful month in Costa Rica during the blissful interim period after one state job ended and before the next one was scheduled to begin. I stayed with my sweetie at Airbnbs in Italy and Croatia when we weren't living on a sailboat. Small trips, large trips... I couldn't imagine staying in a hotel anymore. Meanwhile, I loved to open my little fairytale home to friends. I hosted gatherings all the time. I had thought, occasionally, about getting a roommate, but I really didn't want a roommate... Roommates have stuff. Roommates move in.

Instead, I wanted guests! Guests who are on vacation. Guests who are delighted to be here. Guests who are pre-screened and pre-paid, neat and tidy, and who follow the house rules. Guests who, as it turned out, ended up being the best benefit to being an Airbnb host, because they are so WONDERFUL TO MEET!

Oh, I could tell you stories...

1

Dining room windows at the Little Purple House

Part 1: Air - the Vibe

SOMETIMES, A PLACE ITSELF IS FULL OF MAGIC. It may be some special features of the house that capture your imagination, or the beauty of the property it rests on. Perhaps the surrounding landscape is what draws you in, or the historical significance of the setting. However it happens, there can be a quality in the "air" of some places that can be magical, delightful, and unforgettable.

The following stories from my guests, from my own experiences as a host, and from other local hosts share this central theme: that the "air" of a place can transform an ordinary vacation or visit into something extraordinary and special.

"I was looking to find somewhere to stay in the Twin Cities where I could cook Thanksgiving dinner for family and friends AND where I could bring my three dogs. I had just about given up hope until I found Trudy. I don't even know where to begin to describe this experience. From our first contact until goodbyes, Trudy did everything she could to make my family feel at home. Sweet little touches like dog biscuits for the pups, coffee, tea and snacks for the humans.

Trudy's home is a magical place. Once you arrive you don't want to leave. You immediately feel a sense of place and peace and home. It's a great little neighborhood with an inviting pub down the street and a wonderful park across the street where we could walk the dogs. There are too many positives to mention. The only negative was having to say goodbye. Thank you Trudy. You are one of a kind."

Like The Locals Do

I GREW UP IN SAINT PAUL, MINNESOTA, A COUPLE OF MILES FROM WHERE I'M CURRENTLY LIVING. It's a big small town – people who grew up here tend not to leave. Or, like me, they return someday. There's a friendly rivalry with the other half of the Twin Cities across the Mississippi River. Minneapolis is more like a small big city.

The view from Indian Mounds Park

I took this photo on my way downtown one morning, when the coolness of the fall air met the still-warm waters of the Mississippi and the city was enveloped in a blanket of fog. A deer, coming up from the river bluff, stood at attention by the side of the road. I love my neighborhood, high on the bluff.

For my guests, I have a big binder with dozens of professionally-produced maps and guides. I also stuff the binder with coupons, menus from local restaurants, and my own hand-compiled notes. For an artist couple from Chicago, I created a list of interesting galleries. Want to see the eagle's nest 2 blocks away? I drew a map for that. Want to walk to the farmer's market? Mapped out. Want a nice 4-mile running route? In the binder. When I travel, I want to get to know the place like the locals do.

Turns out, I'm not the only one who thinks that way.

A Warm Welcome

ZUZU, THE FURRY SAMOYED, WAS A BORN HOSTESS.

Loving everyone and everything, she greeted one and all with the sure knowledge that she was loved in return.

"Trudy - thank you for sharing your wonderful home with us this week. We have definitely found a "home away from home" with you and Zuzu.

The wedding was gorgeous and memorable, but we'll never forget your kindness in giving us an oasis from the excitement. Peace and love to you."

Zuzu (2003 - 2017)

5

Photo of Sarina in Bosnia

Hans and I

Sarina, Host of "DREAMY Chic Apartment" www.airbnb.com/rooms/1042159

WHEN HANS AND I FIRST COMMUNICATED THROUGH THE AIRBNB WEBSITE IT WAS IMMEDIATELY CLEAR THAT WE WERE KINDRED SPIRITS. The language barrier between us was obvious, but the commonalities in worldview, personal preference and appreciation for life seemed to make that situation sort of charming — funny at times. I will never forget his writing that he had a "huge brain" when it came to organization but also a "pea brain" when it came to remembering the difference between Tuesday and Thursday. This total stranger made me laugh from the get-go.

The deal was struck - he would stay at my flat while I was in Bosnia.

Hans was traveling from Hamburg, Germany to Saint Paul in June to attend a conference at the University of Minnesota, just minutes from my neighborhood. At 46, he had never traveled outside of Europe. When he saw the pictures of my little yard and flat, he wrote and told me he wanted to stay at my "little paradise," but wondered how he should go about finding transportion to the University each day.

When I explained, in writing, that I lived 3 blocks from the train, a European staple, Hans wrote back that he had found his perfect spot in America. The deal was struck – he would stay at my flat while I was in Bosnia.

Fast-forward a few months. Hans and I are texting daily while he is in Minnesota and I am abroad. We shared the surprises and awe at traveling in a foreign country. I showed him pictures of the Bosnian pyramids and whined of eating too much fresh baked bread while he shared tales of trying to understand 'Minnesota nice' and eating his first fried cheese curd. When he was finished in Minnesota, I suggested he travel to the Grand Canyon before departing the States. He did this and said when he saw it he wept at the beauty of it all.

Hans and I still have not met. He has stayed at my flat twice more since then and has seen New York City, Houston and New Orleans. (The last one was my suggestion.)

Drawing of Tess's kitchen by her guest: Patricia Jacques

Tess's Z Marmalade

Tess, Host of "Sweet Room, Historic Home" www.airbnb.com/rooms/317499

I DON'T ALWAYS GIVE PEOPLE MY SECRET RECIPE. I sometimes offer my guests tart cherry marmalade from my cherry tree or currant jelly from my currant bushes. I have the jar of Tess's Z marmalade in my hand while I look at the guests in front of me and decide whether to offer the Z marmalade to them instead. Sometimes they really need to be cheered up and they need to have their mind taken off what's going on. They may be here for their father's fourth wedding. Or they may be here because their mother has Alzheimer's and needs to be moved. Or there may have been a death in the family. Or, if they are just very playful and I can tell that they like games. That's when I bring out the Z marmalade.

I tell them, "Here's a game you can play. You can turn it down. Here's a jar of the Z marmalade. If you guess the main ingredient, I'll give you a dollar. If you can't guess, then you give me a dollar." And they don't know what to say. Sometimes they laugh. One guy just handed me a dollar, and he said "Okay, here's a dollar, just tell me." I replied, "No, that's not a game. Not doing it."

I tell them, "Here's a game you can play. You can turn it down."

You have to taste the marmalade. There's ginger and oranges in it, but they're a small part of what the marmalade is. It's delicious! People ask for the recipe and I give it to them. One guest wrote in my guest book: "For future guests – I just want to tell you that the secret ingredient is ▨▨▨▨." And then wrote: "Feel free to block for future guests."

My guests have taken the marmalade to a restaurant and had their grandchildren guess, and have then passed it on to the waiter to have his help. They write to me about it later, or tell me about it during their stay. It's really fun!

The Z marmalade becomes part of the experience that many of my guests have when they stay with me.

"Thanks for taking my dollar. It was delicious. You have a lovely place, and you are a marvelous person. That is all."

Tess's jams

"I've stayed in many places in the Twin Cities over the past five years, but it was a real treat to reside here for a few days. You can't imagine a more ideal location.

The surrounding quaint neighborhood is filled with exquisite old homes that would please any architecture buff, and this particular house is decorated with impeccable style. The garden is quite peaceful, and Tess's bees produce truly delicious honey, which she offers along with a vast array of teas, some of which she grew herself. Her jams and marmalades are something else, and I wish you the best of luck in trying to guess her secret ingredient.

Last but certainly not least, Tess is an incredibly charming host who is very knowledgeable about the history of the area, and she can make lots of recommendations to suit your interests.

She's half the reason to stay here, and after spending a few days talking to her I really want her to invite me on her upcoming trip to Albania! Our communication was a breeze, and she was very flexible with my changing arrival times.

After such a lovely experience, I obviously intend to stay here again."

Tess's bee hives - 'the girls'

11

Driveway poppy

Imperfection

I ASKED MY NEIGHBOR TO HOLD OFF ON MOWING THE STRIP OF GRASS AND WEEDS BETWEEN OUR DRIVEWAYS THIS SPRING. "Just wait," I told him. "Let the weeds grow. It will be okay, I promise."

Reluctantly, he agreed. Dandelions soon thrived in the narrow space. The grass grew taller. Other weeds crowded in. It was a mess. Truly.

However, I could see, rising up like fuzzy alien pods on slender stalks, the reason for my insistence on clutter. First one, then another, and then a glorious chaos of the deepest orange burst into bloom as poppies POPPIES came into being.

How gorgeous they are. If I had been more intent on perfection and control, I would have mowed them down.

There is a lot to be said for imperfection.

"Trudy - My daughter found you and your wonderful home for us to stay and I am so glad that she did. It is a magical little kingdom. The house and its beautiful artwork leave a new thing to enjoy at every turn.

But the garden - it is just my favorite because each part is natural but perfect as though Mother Nature took her best ideas and surrounded your house and your carriage house with them. It was such a pleasure to be here, to meet you and your welcoming committee (Zuzu). Thanks for sharing your kingdom!

Your kindred spirit."

"Dear Trudy and Zuzu - If I listed every wonderful, delightful thing about this place you've created you'd have to buy a new guest book! Suffice it to say, we will always remember our getaway here, and we'll tell our new baby all about it after she arrives in August!

If you're ever in Wyoming or Georgia, let us know!"

Air Be & Me

Photo of living room at "Minnestay" by Lance

14

I Could Show You All These Great Places

Lance, Host of "Minnestay - Urban Oasis in Uptown Minneapolis" www.airbnb.com/rooms/19790949

I REMEMBER ONE GUEST WHO CAME TO TOWN AND STAYED WITH ME FOR JUST TWO DAYS IN JUNE. She arrived from Chicago by bus. Once she was settled in at the house, I gave her some recommendations for restaurants close by, and she set off to explore the city.

The next morning, while we were talking over coffee, I realized that she didn't know anyone in the Twin Cities except me. She was in town to attend the Gay Pride Festival. She asked me about bus schedules and how to get downtown. She was interested in my suggestions for places she should visit while she was here. I threw it out there that I could show her the town. I asked her, "Why don't we go and do Minneapolis? I could show you all these great places, and you can see the city."

The next morning, while we were talking over coffee, I realized that she didn't know anyone in the Twin Cities except me.

We toured Uptown together and drove around Lake Calhoun. Then I took her downtown to the Festival and dropped her off there. Later that evening, when she returned to the house, she talked about the parade and how awesome it was. She commented on how much she loved Minneapolis and the people here.

At the end of her stay, I brought her to the bus station and said "goodbye."

Lovely gal. Fun to talk to.

"Lance made me feel welcomed. The place looked exactly like it did in the pictures. This was my first Airbnb stay, and I definitely felt safe and comfortable even though this was a new place. This was very important because I was solo on this trip."

15

Photo of "Little Red Cardinal Home" by Deb

Little Red Cardinal Home

Deb, Host of "Little Red Cardinal Home" www.airbnb.com/rooms/20757487

CARDINALS HAVE LONG BEEN KNOWN BY NATIVE AMERICANS TO SPIRITUALLY SYMBOLIZE A MESSENGER COMING FORTH ACROSS CULTURES AND BELIEFS. They also symbolize good health, happy relationships, and protection. Cardinal's intense red plume and their 'pay attention' chirps seem to mark an importance of some kind that I can't quite put my finger on. It is for this reason that we named our house 'The Little Red Cardinal Home.'

Cardinals had not normally mingled among our typical feathered crew at the feeder, yet a few years ago they showed up one day to devour our sunflower supply and they haven't left since. Every time I see a cardinal I believe something special is about to happen. It is for this reason that I find the name of our house truly mirrors our Airbnb visitations. Something special certainly does happen when guests arrive.

It is through my dealings with Airbnb folks, however, that my faith in the goodness of mankind has begun to grow in a way I never expected.

With a turbulent world raging in every nook and cranny it's easy to shy away from the human population with dark thoughts of what could happen if we allow a stranger into our home. We lock our doors, pull the shades, and sometimes do everything we can to shut out what seems to be a dangerous world. It is through my dealings with Airbnb folks, however, that my faith in the goodness of mankind has begun to grow in a way I never expected.

One such 'messenger,' an engaged couple from down South, visited our Wisconsin home. Possibly it was because we missed our own grown children, or perhaps it was purely because they were delightful kids who needed help, but my husband and I had a marvelous time getting to know them. We invited them to eat dinner with us each night, which I might add isn't something that a normal Airbnb host usually takes on. As we broke bread together, they spoke about what it was like living in a warmer climate and some of their local customs (like gigging or spearing fish and noodling catfish out of a hole in the lake). We even watched some internet videos on gigging and noodling with them and had a good laugh.

As a Wisconsinite, my husband took his turn and showed off a local restaurant's spicy ghost pepper chicken wings (affection-ately called '666 Wings'). We talked about deer and turkey hunting, ice fishing, snowmobiling/ skiing/tobogganing in the snow, and cow tipping.

Our cozy living room was a perfect place to answer questions about my love of writing and the books I've published. Through these conversations, we formed a bond, and we could easily see that even though we're from different parts of the country, we really weren't that different at all. When the couple was ready to leave, I realized just how deep a connection had been formed, and I doubt it will be forgotten by either side.

Airbnb vacationers made me think of the old days when it was quite common for travelers to stay with folks as they traversed from town to town. As progress has a way of forging ahead, I imagine that is why hotels were created – they were open 24/7,

Through these conversations, we formed a bond, and we could easily see that even though we're from different parts of the country, we really weren't that different at all.

available near regularly traveled paths, and easy for travelers to rent. But, in my mind, something is missing when you stay at a hotel. You miss the personal connections, the rich history of the area and its natives that isn't written in books or travel pamphlets, and the smallest of unique details that create spectacular memories. You just don't get that from renting a room in a sterilized hotel.

So, when you ask me if I like being an Airbnb host, I would tell you straight up that it's one of the best experiences I've ever had. I get to share a little piece of my family, my pets, and my home with strangers who will likely be lifelong friends.

As far as I'm concerned, our cardinals can continue to bring these messengers to our little country home. The world needs a little more trust and intangible beauty.

So, when you ask me if I like being an Airbnb host, I would tell you straight up that it's one of the best experiences I've ever had.

Deb (writing as Debbra Anne) has authored three books: *The Enlightened Cat*; *Don't Quit Yet: How to Handle Co-Worker Friction with Tenacity, Humor, and Grace*; and *Jam It On: Farm-Fresh Recipes that Transform Jam, Jelly, and Preserves into Unique Meals*. For more information visit www.DebbraAnne.com.

Photo by Deb

Guest drawing of Yukiko

Sanctuary

I ARRIVED HOME, ONE FINE DAY IN APRIL, TO FIND A REMARKABLE DRAWING OF YUKIKO ON THE KITCHEN CHALK BOARD. Blue eyes, white fur, and yes... claws. That's my girl. The kitten, herself, was snuggling in a lap nearby. Sweet little girl, that Yuki-child. She found sanctuary.

The family visiting was looking for sanctuary of their own. The dad's father was in the slow process of dying at the senior center down the block. The family had been staying with relatives, but sorely needed healing. Normalcy. Comfort. The kind of comfort that comes on four padded feet and softly dulls your grief as you focus on the gentle meditation of petting the animal that has claimed your lap.

The funeral was planned, rushed as such planning always is, over Chinese takeout at the dining room table. Variations of Ave Maria made their debut on the piano in the search for the right key. Photos were selected. Shirts ironed.

I came home in the evening after the funeral to find the family gathered in the living room, a small white kitten in the lap of the newly-made widow. Yuki snuggled closer, not a claw in sight.

She gave sanctuary. Good girl.

The funeral was planned, rushed as such planning always is, over Chinese takeout at the dining room table.

"Trudy, thank you for providing a home that both comforted and delighted us. We felt at home and at peace. You are a thoughtful host, and we appreciate that you went out of your way to welcome us, an exhausted and grieving family.

Thank you for the animal therapy!"

Photo of "The Manor" by Trey Fortner

A Place Out of Time

Sean, Host of "The Manor" www.airbnb.com/rooms/317499

FOUR YEARS AGO, I WROTE AN EMAIL TO "TO WHOM IT MAY CONCERN" AT AIRBNB. I asked if they would consider adding my listing to their Spookiest Houses collection. They agreed, and used this picture (left) as the cover shot.

The next year, I decided to look it up to see if it was still posted. Not only was it posted, but I found two other websites that had picked the story up and re-blogged it. Year three, I looked it up again, and I saw over a dozen different places that had mentioned my house. Yahoo, Forbes, Marie Claire… just scads of them. Many had just copied and pasted the original article. Others just made things up (such as the cemetery in the back yard) that I am not aware of!

There is mystery behind the house, including a ghost story.

At one time, long before I owned the house, it was voted the most mysterious house in Saint Paul, Minnesota. There is mystery behind the house, including a ghost story. I've done research on the house and have copies of many original documents. Plus, I met with the family whose ancestors built the house back in 1883 and lived in it for three generations. They owned much of the land in the neighborhood and built many of the houses nearby.

That third year, I was interviewed and the house was toured extensively by NHK public television from Japan. Now, I get about 2,000 views in a month on Airbnb. The listing having gone "viral" has sent me quite a bit of business. Along with the extra attention on the Internet, I've been a SuperHost on Airbnb for about three years now, meaning I consistently get great reviews from my guests.

There have been so many people (over 750) who have stayed at my house over the past years. Scorch, my dog, has been with me the whole time. She is really good

23

with meeting people. Scorch breaks the mold for a Doberman. She doesn't know any visual boundaries. It doesn't matter what color you are, what uniform you wear – she loves everybody. Everybody, that is, as long as they are properly introduced!

We just had a wedding – about twelve people – which went very well. I made sure that I went over and above the call of duty for them. For the event, I was able to get a truck-full of flowers still fresh from a job that a florist friend had done.

I feel more like a steward than an owner. My name might be on the deed, but the house has got a hold of my chain.

Over the years, I've made lifelong friends through Airbnb. One gal has stayed as my guest twelve times now. She knows my place and knows my friends on a first-name basis. That's a friendship that has developed over time. I feel like it's more than just a client relationship. Probably 15% of my clientele end up being my friends on Facebook. It's not like I want to have every single person end up being my Facebook friend, but when you can tell there's a special connection… boom!

Airbnb has made me a better person. I keep a clean house now. A good portion of my house is spotless and it has to be. I didn't used to do that before. Also, now I watch the neighborhood. I call the city about trash. I clean my street at least weekly. In many ways, hosting helped me become a better person. I'm less stressed. I'm healthier because of it.

Photo of Scorch by Trey Fortner

I've lived here ten years and have renovated most of the house. It's been a labor of love. The home has had a facelift inside and out. With all the trees and greenery, you can't really see the neighbors. It feels like you're out in the country, when in fact you're in the middle of the city. If you knew me before I bought the house, you would understand why I bought this house and have worked to make it even more spooky.

Halloween is my favorite holiday. I was a costumer and designed costumes and fashion for many years. Halloween is one of the biggest events of the year for me. So, when I saw this house, I liked it but I waited. I wanted to make sure it wouldn't be an impulse buy. I waited. Later, of course, I bought it.

I feel more like a steward of this house than an owner. My name might be on the deed, but the house has got a hold of my chain.

The place has charm. It has an energy.

It feels like a place out of time.

"Everything we hoped it to be and more. Sean is a fantastic host. Kind, thoughtful and creative. Scorch is a magical creature. It became clear in the first few moments she has been raised with love and kindness. Her kind, calm behavior tells volumes about Sean's commitment to doing things the right way. The same applies to the condition and restoration of his home. Thanks, Sean and Scorch. Very happy our paths crossed. Hope you have a room available during my next trip to St. Paul. "

"Staying at Sean's home was amazing. His creativity radiates out of him into his home, and it makes for a truly unique getaway experience. Scorch is such a sweet pup. We would be back just to hang with her and Sean. Great conversation with him too. Highly recommended. "

25

Photo of entry to "Garden Apartment with a Fireplace" by Nora Farrell

A Space of Love

Tea, Host of "Garden Apartment with a Fireplace" www.Airbnb.com/rooms/10056547

TWO COUPLES TOLD ME THAT THEY HAD SPONTANEOUS ENGAGEMENTS IN MY SPACE! They said that they felt so comfortable and that the space was so romantic with the walk-through couple-friendly shower with the heated floors, the fireplace, and the tempur-pedic mattress... I was very flattered by their engagements, because it's a space of love.

It had been my son's bedroom and my son has since passed away. I love that now lots of people stay in it. Many people are happy there. It was a special space to both my son and me.

I was so flattered by their engagements, because it's a space of love.

In both in my Colorado listing and in my Minneapolis place, I've had people help me discover things that I didn't know about my own neighborhood. In Colorado, a guest told me that she had just gone on the most amazing hike. She said that she walked there from my condo. I had thought I knew all the hikes, but I didn't know this one. She gave me detailed directions, which now I give to other people. It's really cool how you learn things from each other, and then pass this information on, up and down the people chain. I pass information and tips on to other hosts, and they pass their secrets to me. Later, I in turn pass these things on to my guests.

It's also been fun to stay as a guest at other Airbnbs. I get ideas for things that I can incorporate into my units. We wouldn't think of staying in hotels anymore. There is not only the opportunity to have an experience like we are giving, but we can pick up tips everywhere we go.

Photo by Nora Farrell

Three muffins left... for now

Simple Things Matter

WHEN GUESTS MAKE A RESERVATION TO STAY AT MY LITTLE PURPLE HOUSE, I WANT THEM TO HAVE AN AMAZING EXPERIENCE. I ask them about their food preferences - are they gluten-free? Do they tolerate dairy? Then I stock the fridge and snack basket accordingly.

I always have severals types of coffees, dozens of teas, and a selection of juices on hand. If they don't have specific dietary concerns, I'll also have bagels, cream cheese, half & half, yogurts, biscotti, granola bars, and dark chocolates. If they do avoid some foods, this might translate to gluten-free granola bars and crackers, almond milk, fresh fruit, nuts, and dark chocolates. Just about everyone eats dark chocolates. Depending on the guests, I also have some local beers and sometimes a bottle of wine for them.

I had one guest who let me know that she couldn't eat gluten, eggs, dairy, or sugar. Poor dear! That first morning I baked oat bran muffins loaded with organic fruits and made without eggs. She was delighted… and I was happy to know that she would never forget her breakfast or her stay.

Simple things matter. When it's possible to go above and beyond to make someone's day, just do it. I don't generally cook for my guests, and I never charge them for food, but quite often have found myself sharing morning coffee with them as we converge at the backyard patio. There have been countless conversations, over a beer and/or a barbecue, where we bring what we have to the table and connect through shared space, shared food, and shared humanity.

"Dear Trudy and Zuzu,

Thank you for your RADICAL HOSPITALITY that went above and beyond all our expecations! Your home is *amazing* - and we loved all of your special extra touches, including the inspiring quotes, the fixtures, and the beautiful stained glass windows!

Thank you for letting our yorkies, Izzy and Emmy, stay here with us, too. It was a perfect retreat-like getaway far from the stresses of everyday life!

The muffins - no dairy, sugar, egg, or gluten - were over-the-top outstanding!! They will be a gift that keeps on giving!

We hope to visit again in the future!"

29

Photo of "New Luxurious Apartment Near Convention Center" by Tyler

Making Someone's Day

Tyler, Host of "New Luxurious Apartment Near Convention Center" www.airbnb.com/rooms/18754468

ONE OF THE MORE ENJOYABLE EXPERIENCES I'VE HAD WITH A GUEST WAS WITH A GREEK PHYSICIAN COUPLE. They were looking for a place where they could stay for almost a full month while they explored Minnesota with their two children and found a home in Minnesota near their new jobs.

Many, many logistics went wrong for this family as they were trying to plan their trip, but we were able to help resolve the situation each time. Once they arrived and were settled in to their apartment, things went a lot smoother for them.

We had a four-hour dinner, sharing stories about Greece, global politics, and their stay in Minneapolis. It was a blast!

We kept in touch during their stay and before they left, they asked if they could have dinner with my staff, who had helped them out in a number of ways. I brought the whole team. We went out to a great steak and burger place that has been in Minneapolis for decades. We had a four hour dinner, sharing stories about Greece, global politics, and their stay in Minneapolis.

It was a blast!

I am a serial entrepreneur. I have other businesses. However, what makes me most proud of what my team and I are accomplishing is when I pull up our Airbnb reviews and see the stories from people who say that this is the best Airbnb experience they have ever had. We always try to add those little extras that make a difference.

Those little details matter.

It's so cool to see how you can really make someone's day.

Photos of flowers from the author's garden by Airbnb guest #JaadinAdeleStudio

"Trudy -It takes a special person to create a home like this one and an even more special one to open it up to strangers.

I wish the world was filled with kind and generous people like you. Your gardens made me think of my Mom who has just begun to heal from a regimen of chemo/radiation. She is a gardener, and you can feel her soul out there.

Like you, she makes the inside of her home garden-like, too. I will share pictures with her next week and tell her about this special place where strangers become housemates and even dogs are welcome."

Trust and unlikely friendships

Part 2: Be(longing)

W E ARE BOMBARDED DAILY WITH MESSAGES THAT THE WORLD IS FULL OF BAD PEOPLE WHO DO TERRIBLE THINGS TO EACH OTHER. We turn on our TVs and hear reports of the latest crimes; we open our Facebook feeds to scenes of political and social disconnection. Numbed, we begin to believe the world is full of danger. That it is safer to shut ourselves off. To communicate through our devices. To fear.

Except that somehow, in the midst of this division and distrust, people across the planet have begun to open their homes to strangers. Think about it. What kind of trust does it take to welcome a complete stranger into your personal space?

This home sharing happens every day, on a massive scale, around the world. Airbnb hosts and guests have recognized that the vast majority of humans are good, decent, and trustworthy people. This platform provides an avenue for people to connect meaningfully with each other. From a global perspective, this is no longer merely transactional. This is transformational.

There is a gentle revolution that is being staged in homes and livingrooms across the globe. We conquer fear by learning trust. We rid the world of strangers when we turn them into friends.

There Is A Chemistry

Stephanie, Host of "Cozy top floor with a great view" www.Airbnb.com/rooms/4854087

IT ALWAYS WORKS OUT, BUT IT DOESN'T ALWAYS WORK OUT PERFECTLY. I have found the people who use Airbnb to be largely trusting, kind and grateful for the opportunity to stay in my home. But like any experience, there is a wide cross section of folks who choose to stay with us. Some are quirky, some are quiet, and some are truly friends I hadn't met before (like the ones that stayed with us three times and invited us to their wedding).

We have two cats widely believed to have the souls of dogs who welcome and forge a bond with almost everyone. One evening, my husband and I got home and could hear a cat upstairs in the guest space meowing and calling out. This happens sometimes if they get stuck in a room or a closet. I didn't know if the guests were home so I knocked on the door to the upstairs, called out "hello, anyone home?"

> When you welcome people into your home, there are the facts of where the bathroom is and how does the coffee maker work, but there is also a chemistry.

and waited for an answer. No answer was forthcoming, so I went upstairs to release the cat and to my surprise, saw that the guests were sound asleep in their bed! Praying desperately that I wouldn't wake these guests and have to explain why I was creeping around in their bedroom while they were asleep, I headed back downstairs.

Of course, the most common question I get from people who learn that I regularly welcome strangers into my home as guests is "What is the worst experience you've had?"

When you welcome people into your home, there are the facts of where the bathroom is and how does the coffee maker work, but there is also a chemistry. The result is always a mystery. There are the people that feel like they are the friends you haven't met yet and you wish they would stay longer. Those are the people that we invite to join us for dinner or breakfast and for whom we make plans to visit.

But there are also the people that for whatever reason avail themselves of our hospitality, are cordial, and then are on their way. This is not a fail; it is a fact. It distills the basics of our arrangement down to a financial and logistical one. These people needed a place to stay and we had a place for them to stay. It's not wrong, it's just real.

There was the guest we never met. He had reserved our space and learned on the day of check-in (when he entered our address into his navigation system) that he was 1000 miles away. Woodbury New York instead of Woodbury Minnesota, as it happens.

But for every guest who was just fine, there is a guest who is more than fine. A guest who is someone you feel that you would like to know better or have the vague sense that you would be friends if they didn't live in another state or country.

So whenever anyone asks about 'horrible experiences' I always reply that while many of our guests are fine, many are more than fine - delightful in fact, but none are horrible.

There was the woman who wanted to sit in living room all day Saturday and Sunday to watch the golf channel. You can guess which category she falls into.

I think that is the essence of the Airbnb experience for me: it's not the predictable and sterile nature of a hotel. It's an interesting, sometimes messy opportunity to have an interaction with another imperfect human being.

Photos by Thomas, Stephanie's guest

37

Air Be & Me

Photo of Saint Paul skyline by Steven Mosborg, www.MosborgExposures.com

38

More Connection in this World

Jenessa, Host of "Lovely Studio Minutes from Downtown"

AIRBNB CHANGED MY LIFE. I started travelling with Airbnb when I was studying in Montpelier, in southern France. I had travelled around Europe quite a bit, since I'm Italian-American, but had made some American friends at school who wanted to see Europe for the first time. Many Europeans are Airbnb hosts, so we could easily find affordable places to stay. For the most part, we rented whole apartments and had minimal interaction with our hosts. However, in Munich, we rented a place where there was a long-term renter in the other room. He and the owner, Oosman, were both very sweet people. At the end of my stay, I gave Oosman a wine glass from Montpelier. I didn't think anything of it, but in his review of me he went on and on about how nice we were and how much he appreciated the wine glass that I had left. Somehow, this really touched me: how I was able to make this very personal connection with an Arabic person in Germany whom I would have never met in my normal life.

> I started to realize who I really am and what is important to me, and how those personal interactions completely changed my experience spent visiting a place, and shaped how things were going to be there.

I went on to stay at Airbnbs in the United States. In New York, I ended up staying with someone (Andrew) for whom it was his very first time hosting with Airbnb. To this day, Andrew and I are still in touch. When I was there, I had the flu and basically just stayed in my room with Nyquil while my friends were out. Andrew was so kind to me. Now, we talk constantly. We're Facebook friends and we update each other on our lives. He gave me all kinds of advice when I first started hosting with Airbnb.

In other Airbnbs, where I didn't interact as much with the hosts, I still enjoyed my visits but it wasn't the same. I started to realize who I really am and what is important to me, and how those personal interactions completely changed my experience spent visiting a place and shaped how things were going to be there. I also realized that some people really didn't want the interaction, while others did.

I knew I did. I wanted this connection.

So, with my former housemates, I started hosting Airbnb a few years ago. I remember one recently retired woman who stayed with us on her way down to Mexico. We are all sitting down to dinner together, talking with this older traveler about her new adventures, when I realized that you really can re-invent yourself at any age.

People ask: Isn't it weird to have someone in your home? And I say, "No. It's weird to have a life that's closed off to people."

Eventually, I came to understand that it was critical for me to have the connections that come through sharing a home. I moved to my current apartment and began Airbnb hosting on my own. I moved so that I could share my space and create community. I wanted a place that was inviting. Now in my apartment I have artwork that my friends or I made. I've purchased furniture from people who are local. I have placed my grandmother's couch in the livingroom. I want my home to be a place where people feel they are welcomed. Everything about the apartment symbolizes community and sharing.

There was one person in particular who I will never forget because she changed my life. I had a couple traveling from Germany who were going to stay with me. The woman grew up here and her partner was German. She was bringing him here to show him the Twin Cities and to meet her parents.

She asked me if I would be able to drop off the keys at her parents' house. When I arrived there, they welcomed me into their home. They had made cookies and had a big spread there. They said that they were glad to meet me. They asked me questions about my school and my life. Before I knew it, I was rambling on about the big decisions I was wrestling with. I was going to school to be a dentist but had a love of the arts. I didn't know how I could combine the two. It turned out that the woman had been a career counselor for 30 years!

As we talked, I started to realize the freedom that I have in my choices. It was an incredible

Photo of "Lovely Studio" by Jenessa

conversation. I left their house two hours later, having only planned to dropped off keys. From that moment on I started down a new path in my life. I had figured out what to do with my life. What I wanted to be when I grew up.

It was so beautiful. The couple ended up staying at my place for a week. Every day, they would send me pictures from the places I had recommended that they visit. It was incredible. There is nothing better than to realize that you have helped to make someone's visit special.

We all have similar needs and part of that is belonging.

I'll always think about that moment in my life. That I had been so unhappy with my career choice, and that my whole trajectory changed because of one conversation with someone that I would otherwise never have met.

There needs to be more connection in this world. People who will open up their homes and be there for each other. People ask, "Isn't it weird to have someone in your house?" And I say, "No. It's weird to have a life that's closed off to people." That is denying so much of who we are. We all have similar needs and part of that is belonging.

Why do we isolate ourselves from each other?

There have been so many times when I've gone home to my family and have said to them, "I've just had this conversation with somebody from Airbnb, and I have to tell you about it."

My family has seen how it has changed my life.

I feel so blessed.

Metal sculpture in author's yard

A symbol of trust and community: the author's Little Free Library

Re-Learning Trust

I REMEMBER BEING NERVOUS BEFORE NATHAN CAME TO VISIT. I was staying in the house at the time, renting out my guest room, and Nathan was the first single male I had allowed in. Even though he had great reviews from his previous experiences as a guest on Airbnb, I still worried...

The review system that Airbnb has is a wonderful resource for hosts. We can read reviews about our potential guests that help us understand if they can be trusted. Needless to say, I'm so glad I let Nathan stay. My trust was completely rewarded with kindness and gratitude.

We read and listen to horror stories about uncommon events that do not accurately reflect reality. Most people are truly good and kind, just like we are.

We need to re-learn trust.

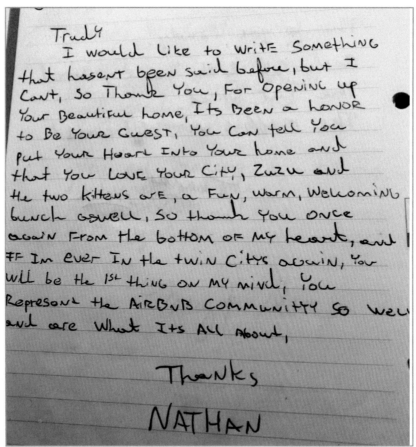

> Trudy
> I would like to write something that hasent been said before, but I cant, so Thank You, For Opening up Your Beautiful home, Its Been a honor to Be Your Guest, You Can tell You put Your Heart Into Your home and that You Love Your City, Zuzu and the two kittens are, a Fun, warm, Welcoming bunch aswell, So thank You once again From the bottom of My heart, and If Im ever In the twin Citys again, You will be the 1st thing on My mind, You Represent the AiRBnB Community so well and are What Its All About,
>
> Thanks
> NATHAN

Photo of her back yard by Christine

Exchanging Cultures

Christine, Host of "Casa de Barajas" www.airbnb.com/rooms/5959182

A COUPLE OF YEARS AGO, A GENTLEMAN CONTACTED ME ABOUT STAYING AT MY HOUSE — BUT HE ASKED A LOT OF STRANGE QUESTIONS. "Do you serve breakfast?" And, "How far are you from the hospital?"

This guest was from Lebanon. He was coming to study to be a doctor. Only students in the top percentile of their class were even considered to be able to go outside of Lebanon to continue their studies. He was definitely the pride and joy of his family and was very conscientious of spending his family's money. He was determined to make the most of his studies while he was here in Minnesota.

We would sit down together for dinner so that he could get to try different types of food.

The program that he was enrolled in was all about understanding what was expected by Americans regarding a physician's bedside manner. Doctors in Lebanon are completely different – much more God-like. As a patient, you do what they say, and don't ask questions.

We offered to pick him up at the airport, since this was his first trip to the United States. He was friendly, fun, and spoke perfect English. On the way home from the airport, we took him to Mercado Centrale to have a beer and allow him to choose from different foods. We ate tacos there – he had never had them before. The next day, we took him to the grocery store because he was very concerned about being able to buy bread. When we walked into the store, he was totally relieved that there would be bread available. However, when we arrived at the bread aisle, he was completely overwhelmed at the choices of different kinds of bread. We spent some time finding a bread that was most similar to the breads he was used to in Lebanon.

I would often times cook for him, and we would sit down together for dinner so

that he would get to try different types of food. However, we learned that we needed to help him with some basic skills that men tend to know in the U.S., but aren't expected to know in Lebanon. For example, he didn't know how to cook. He didn't know how to do laundry.

He was studying at Hennepin County Medical Center. He had a big book of scenarios of different patients and their symptoms. In the evenings, we would practice these scenarios together. I would read up on who I was supposed to be (an old man with chest pain, etc.), and he would need to ask me questions to figure out my condition. But first, he would need to greet me properly, look me in the eye, introduce himself, and explain what he was going to do: "I'm going to listen to your heart." Little things mattered, like how he covered you up, made sure he washed his hands before he touched you, and so on. All the things that doctors are trained to do here, but might not have learned elsewhere.

It was the middle of a cold Minnesota winter and he was not prepared! We loaned him coats and gloves, and made sure he had warm winter clothes to wear.

He covered all the examples in his book, over and over. In one of our first practice interviews, I took the part of a woman patient. He asked a series of questions, and then asked me, "how many abortions have you had?" I just about died! I said, "No, no, no! In this country, you need to ask how many pregnancies have you had. You can also ask, How many live births have you had?" This was the first of many interesting cultural exchanges.

He arrived in the middle of a cold Minnesota winter and he was not prepared! We loaned him coats and gloves, and made sure that he had warm winter clothes to wear. Most of the time, our guest would be studying when he came home from the hospital, but sometimes he would take a break to enjoy Minneapolis. My son had moved home during his senior year at college and would invite our Lebanese guest to hockey games and other events with him. They were pretty close in age and soon became friends. One day, when I was doing the laundry for my husband and me, our guest turned to me and asked, "Why don't you do your son's laundry? I don't understand! You're his mother." This turned into another fascinating discussion about our cultures. There were so many funny things that you didn't realize would be different.

Every day, I learned something new – about his culture and my own. I took him to church, because he had wanted to attend a Lebanese church here. It was so fun to experience a different culture's church! Our guest was a very religious person. In Lebanon, it is very common that the priest will take care of where you are going to stay when you are traveling. He had originally contacted his local priest to find a place to stay in Minneapolis, but then found me

Christine shoveling a path to the hottub

on-line. He read the reviews of how I had helped others become accustomed to how to use the bus, etc., and decided to stay with us.

I wanted to help him be successful here as a doctor, and that meant he would need to understand our culture.

This was a fantastic, fun experience and a growth experience for my family as well as for me. He stayed with us for a month. I wanted to help him be successful here as a doctor, which meant that he would need to understand our culture. Every day, I tried to explain our life to him in ways that would make sense. I talked about the fact that I also worked outside the home, which was not common in his country. I explained why it was important to me that my son be independent, and know how to cook and do his own laundry.

After he finished his program here in Minneapolis, he returned home for another course and then found a position at one of the best medical institutions in the U.S.

We keep in touch through Facebook.

47

Guests heading out to the Minnesota Renaissance Festival

Each Guest Has A Story

OVER THE YEARS, GUESTS HAVE VISITED MY LITTLE PURPLE HOUSE FOR A VARIETY OF REASONS. There was the woman who was competing in the International Women's Flat Track Roller Derby Championship Tournament. To the uninitiated, that's competitive (and somewhat combative) women's roller skating. A few months earlier, a different guest competed in several track events in the Senior Olympics. Both of these women made liberal use of the bath salts.

There was the charming young woman from Arizona who was in town to reunite with her father, whom she had not seen in far too long. They cooked me a Tex-Mex feast as a "thank you." Another booking brought me four sisters in their 70s who lived around the world but converged at my house for a few days one summer to celebrate the eldest's 80th birthday. Another time, a shy young woman from China stayed and studied in my guest bedroom for a month, emerging occasionally to cook a meal before returning to her books.

There was one memorable and delightful group who came to attend the Minnesota Renaissance Festival. Early one morning during their visit, I heard a tentative knock. I opened the door to find a somewhat panicked guest who assured me that an order for the exact replacement for my electric kettle had already been placed on Amazon and would be arriving the next day. When it came, I made sure to put a large label on it that read: "Do NOT place on stovetop." It was, after all, the third electric kettle that guests had purchased for me that year. Haven't had a problem since.

"Trudy - I knew as soon as I saw your beautiful home that we would fall in love with it as much as with our own. Your love of the space speaks in all the details. It's been a wonderful place to come "home" to. My family all lives up here and it meant the world that I could host dinner for my 84 year-old grandma instead of her having the hassle and cleanup. Thank you for giving me the opportunity to host.

Enjoy the new kettle! I hope that you enjoyed having a couple oddly-dressed folks running around before the Renaissance Festival. Thank you more than can be said."

49

Ameet and Tamara

A Very Holistic Way of Becoming Friends

Tamara, Host of "Comfy Room in Eco-Friendly House" www.airbnb.com/rooms/1798035

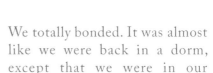

AMEET BEGINS: "I'LL START, BECAUSE I WAS THE GUEST. I had just arrived in Minneapolis a couple days previously. I was able to stay in the first Airbnb for only two days because they had another reservation. I didn't know where to go. I had no idea about the location, and didn't know anything about Minneapolis, but Tamara's place was available. It seemed close to the highway, so I thought I would just try this.

I emailed Tamara and she accepted that I would stay for three weeks. We negotiated a price, which was very sweet. I showed up at Tamara's the next day. I had just started my job at General Mills, and it was pretty taxing in the sense that everything was new. I didn't have a routine. However, Tamara's place was not too small and not too big – it was very conducive to just hang out in. So, every once in a while, I would chat with Tamara and her daughter over morning chai.

We totally bonded. It was almost like we were back in a dorm, except that we were in our late thirties.

As we began talking, we realized we had a lot in common. We had lived in New York at the same time. We are close to the same age, so we have that generational and geographical connection. We totally bonded. It was almost like we were back in a dorm, except that we were in our late 30s."

"Totally like roommates," interjects Tamara, "but in a good way."

Ameet continues: "After 3 ½ weeks, we were going to either hate each other, or love each other. We ended up loving each other. Three and a half years later, we are still friends. I've moved to New York, and Tamara has been to my place many times. We hang out at the beach. She has met my other friends. It's just a good way to get to know someone. The person happens to be your host or your guest, but adults meeting this way would be quite impossible otherwise. Adults forming new friendships like this is quite unheard of, but are possible through Airbnb. You are inviting people into your home, which is a private space. For people who recognize that, and who honor that, there is the potential for these friendships to happen. I definitely give Airbnb the credit for making this happen."

"It was very sweet," comments Tamara. "He would make chai in the morning, while I would be running off to work, and I would have a nice hot cup of chai on my morning commute. It was February and snowing. I remember one time we had 8-12 inches of new snow and I couldn't get my car moving. Ameet came out and helped me push it. We just clicked very easily.

One of the comments that I have heard from Airbnb is that they don't want travel to be a transaction, they want it to be a transformation."

Ameet states, "Because Tamara is a nutritional counselor, I've learned how to take better care of my health. I didn't need to make a doctor's appointment or anything – it was just part of the conversation. It's an unwritten perk – you can gain from your host's talents."

Tamara agrees, "I've since been to Ameet for business advice. Once, I had him read a really important email that I was going to use to create business for my company. It's good to have someone

> Adults forming new friendships like this is quite unheard of, but I think that it is possible through Airbnb, because you are inviting people into your home, which is a private space.

that you know and trust to ask for advice."

Ameet adds "Tamara was my counselor and advisor when I was in a relationship. And I am hers now."

Tamara continues "It doesn't matter if Ameet is in New York, or here. Near or far, we keep in touch and visit each other."

"I would love to buy a place in Minneapolis within the next year," comments Ameet. "I'm sure that if I do, I'll be an Airbnb host at some point, because I'd love also having people over and making new connections. Your lives intersect in such different ways when you are in someone's home. That's a different kind of interaction altogether. It's a very holistic, natural way of becoming friends.

I've been to Airbnbs all around the world. I personally would rather get to know a place through people, rather than by reading a book. Airbnb allows for that interchange, which is quite needed and very good. It doesn't matter whether I'm visiting a city for vacation or to perform as a musician, I still prefer to stay at an Airbnb."

"You get to know and learn a city from the ground level," says Tamara. "You're not going to get that from a hotel concierge. Staying with a host and making that connection, even if it's not lasting, helps you know that you have a trusted friend in town who has your best interests in mind. Someone who wants to help you to feel at home, which is the role of a host. They often serve as an ambassador for their city. This is a huge service that the city doesn't realize. It helps people to return when they feel that there is a warm connection, even if they don't maintain it with that host."

Ameet concludes, "Airbnb hosts have a responsibility. It's more than just being a host."

I personally would rather get to know a place through people, rather than by reading a book.

Tamara's refrigerator offerings

Ameet's music can be heard live at concerts in the Twin Cities and New York, and is also available at www.ameetkamath.com.

Photo of porch area at "Petite Suite"

Repeat Guests

Jayson, Host of "Petite Suite"

W E'VE BEEN HOSTING AIRBNB IN THIS OLD HOUSE IN CATHEDRAL HILL FOR A COUPLE OF YEARS. One thing that has really impressed us is how many people really need an affordable place to stay. They simply couldn't stay at one of the local B&Bs because these are out of their price range. Their other option is to stay at a cheap motel – but then they are way out in the suburbs or in Wisconsin. A lot of people come to our "Petite Suite" because they are in a distance-learning program at one of the local colleges. So, a couple times a year, they come to town for a week or two of classes. We get many repeat guests because of that program.

One thing that has impressed me is how many people really need an affordable place to stay.

One guest has been here several times. In November, it will be her fourth or fifth visit. And every time she comes, she brings a bottle of Iowa-brewed bourbon. My husband just loves the stuff! Last time, she brought this really strong coffee – some sort of double jolt. It was delicious. You start building relationships with guests. They come back.

We keep in contact with her from Iowa between visits. She lets us know what her kids are up to. She always brings us gifts… It's a real relationship now. We were her first experience with Airbnb and she was a little nervous at first. She had contacted us through the site to learn more about the apartment and the area. We wrote back and forth quite a bit, letting her know about things to do in the area. Finally, she had her first stay. Halfway through her first week, our guest had come back from studying at law school. We invited her to join us for a drink at the Commodore – a nearby bar that had been a favorite of F. Scott Fitzgerald and had recently been restored. We walked over as a group. After we got settled in at the bar, we just yakked for two hours straight. Great gal.

55

One of the stained glass windows at "Comfortable Victorian"

They've Adopted Me - Or I've Adopted Them

Susan, Host of "Comfortable Victorian" www.airbnb.com/rooms/4010919

COME THIS NOVEMBER, IT WILL BE FOUR YEARS THAT I HAVE BEEN AN AIRBNB HOST. I got into it because a friend of mine in Minneapolis had started doing it. She called me up and said, "I'm having the best fun!" She added, "You should do this too. You'd be an ideal host."

So, I thought, why not?

There was this one family from the Philippines who first came to stay a couple years back. They wanted to know if they could cook in my kitchen. I said, "Of course you can!" They arrived with their vegetables and their pots and pans (which are still here in the kitchen), and they cooked! At first they asked me: "Is this okay? Is that okay?" I said to them, "The kitchen is yours!"

They make me this wonderful Filipino food. They call to me, "Come and eat, Susan! Come and eat!"

They are Filipino, so when they come, they really bring the family. There's the aunt, the brother, the grandfather, and so on. They have a son going to Macalester University nearby, so they come to visit a couple times a year. They're a hoot! Twice a year now, they just walk in and they cook for me! They make me this wonderful Filipino food. They call to me, "Come and eat, Susan! Come and eat!"

Then we sit outside on the patio till it's dark and eat and talk and talk. There have been occasions when they've wanted to stay with me, but haven't been able to get in because I tend to get booked up well ahead of time. So, they've emailed me and asked if I would like to attend a concert with them while they are in town. And I say, "Yes, of course, I'd love to do that!"

We keep in touch on Facebook. Even after their son graduates, we'll probably stay in contact. They've adopted me. Or, I've adopted them.

Morning glory chair

Unexpected, But Beautiful

A FEW WEEKS AGO, I NOTICED THAT THE MORNING GLORIES HAD TAKEN OVER ONE OF THE CHAIRS AROUND THE FIRE PIT. I hadn't had a fire in weeks. This, apparently, was all the encouragement necessary for these beautiful but persistent invaders.

They had moved in past the strawberries and the basil. Even past the blueberries. Into human spaces. Anchoring the chair to the Earth with strong green cords, waving flags of purple and white.

When did this happen?

I didn't notice the chair yesterday evening, when I joined my guests from Iowa in conversation around the patio table a few steps away. Delightful group: two couples who had known each other for decades. We talked of the challenges of evolving economic drivers; of the disparities that perpetuate between city blocks; of the transformation of neighborhoods that occurs when people from different cultures find new areas to settle.

We talked of the importance of music, old and new.

Meanwhile, behind me, the morning glories were continuing their steady advance into alien territory. New settlers in an established neighborhood, making themselves at home. Unexpected, but beautiful.

We talked of the challenges of evolving economic drivers; of the disparities that perpetuate between city blocks; of the transformation of neighborhoods that occurs when people from different cultures find new areas to settle.

Entry to "Lovely Historic Brownstone"

Plans for The Extra Income

Chris, Host of "Studio in My Lovely Historic Brownstone" www.airbnb.com/rooms/16047707

MY REALITY: AIRBNB HAS KEPT RENT PRICES LOWER FOR MY LONG-TERM TENANTS. I own a historic brownstone in downtown Minneapolis and have long-term tenants whom I love! However, each year, expenses increase from water to commercial liability insurance to property taxes and it goes on and on. Wages have increased for painters and maintenance. Yet I have only modestly increased rents bi-annually a few percent over the years. The minimum rent increases have caused financial strain until Airbnb.

Airbnb allows me to bring in extra income so that I don't have to increase the rents on my existing tenants.

One tenant who started traveling out of town asked if she could short term rent her apartment. I agreed if she shared her net gain after cleaning. She agreed. This allowed me to not have to increase her rent. I then started to rent a studio apt via Airbnb that became available last winter. The increased income on this unit has allowed me to not increase rents in 2017, keeping most of my units to remain under $850/month when typical downtown rentals are deep into the thousands.

At first, I just couldn't believe that so many people were interested in Airbnb as an option other than a hotel. I love these historic buildings and would prefer staying in them to a hotel. Come to find out, there are other people who like these historic buildings like I do.

Airbnb allows me to bring some extra income in so that don't have to increase the rents on my existing long-term tenants.

61

Small kindnesses

We Could Get Into Such Trouble

MY GUESTS FROM NEW YORK LEFT A FEW DAYS AGO. A delightful couple in town to celebrate their grandson's wedding. The family drifted in and out between trips to the rehearsal dinner and newlywed brunch, a joyful group who clearly cherished each other. The house was filled with the sound of children.

At the heart of this gathering was a lovely woman, a self-described former hippie turned grandmother, who regaled me with stories of her home in New York and the neighbors who had lived together in her apartment building for decades. They took care of each other. They knew each other.

> The family drifted in and out between trips to the rehearsal dinner and newlywed brunch, a joyful group who clearly cherished each other.

> "You should come to visit us," she said. "We could get into so much trouble."

After she left, I found the towels neatly laundered and stacked on the dining room table. Yes, we could get into such trouble, she and I.

I think I'll need to start planning a trip out East...

> "Trudy- There are no words to describe how perfect our stay at the Little Purple House has been. It's hard to leave. Besides having the most charming house with all the comfort we needed, getting to meet you has been a huge bonus.
>
> We will miss the place, you, and of course, Zuzu."

63

Statue in Indian Mounds Park as the harvest moon is rising

Inclusivity

I LIVE A BLOCK AWAY FROM INDIAN MOUNDS PARK IN SAINT PAUL. The park is a sacred site on a bluff overlooking the Mississippi River which has several American Indian mound burial sites. I also serve on the board of the Minnesota Humanities Center. It was through this organization that I finally began to understand the rich cultural heritage that I am honored to live next to.

As an Airbnb host, I've had the privilege of opening my home to people from many nationalities and backgrounds. I've hosted guests from the Netherlands who were representing their country in the 'Crashed Ice' athletic event in Saint Paul. Other guests, from Scotland, traveled here to attend the Ryder Cup golf tournament. Countless others, too many to mention, have had their experience of Minnesota and the United States flavored by the unique perspective that can be gained by staying at my Little Purple House.

> It is so easy for me to surround myself with people just like me. That would be a mistake. I've had the most delightful encounters with travelers whom I would never have met if it weren't for Airbnb.

These international guests have broadened my outlook on my world. However, my world view has also been expanded by guests from Minnesota and elsewhere in the United States. It is so easy for me to surround myself with people just like me. That would be a mistake. I've had the most delightful conversations with travelers whom I never would have met if it were not for Airbnb.

Generational differences. Taste in music. Politics. We tend to let these things divide us, but they do not actually define us. What defines us, as individuals, is how we treat each other as humans. Are we considerate? Are we honest? These are qualities that have nothing to do with income levels, religion, ethnicity, or sexual preference. These are the qualities that matter. It is our shared humanity that counts.

It has been a true delight to open my home to the many, many guests from inside and outside the United States who have broadened my outlook on the world.

65

An original in the garden

Part 3: Me... and You

OR THAT IS - Us. That's right - you, me, and the thousands of other individuals who have shared our unique and wonderful homes with strangers and found our world getting friendlier. Us: including the millions of Airbnb guests (myself, my guests, and others) who have trusted the hospitality of people we have never met... and who have been overwhelmed by kindness and generosity.

A good part of what makes Airbnb so special is that our creativity, that wonderful, quirky individuality of both host and guest, shines through with each interaction. I finally have come to consider myself an artist after many years of focusing on more left-brained activities. Hours fly by when I'm immersed in some project in the house, carriage house, or yard. I lose myself in my art. I find my self there as well.

I've included some of my guest's art throughout the book, but there were many more drawings that didn't make it in. The couple of pages that follow are a compilation of some of the many guest drawings I've received.

Enjoy!

Little Purple House and Library

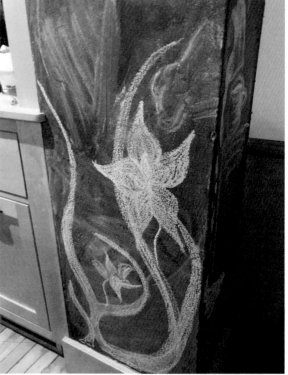

Guest Art Gallery

Guest chalkboard drawing of Zuzu

After Words

As I WRITE THIS, ZUZU HAS BEEN GONE FROM THIS WORLD FOR JUST OVER A WEEK. I'll miss her - she was a good friend for fourteen years. The kitties, Yoshi and Yukiko, were welcomed back several months ago to the home where their biological mother lives. Turns out, I had allergies after all. I miss them, too.

Two of the Airbnb hosts who contributed stories to this book are no longer listing at those addresses, but just last week I met a dozen new potential hosts who were eager to learn the ropes. In time, they will have their own stories to share.

Just as you may have stories to share.

If you've been hosting or staying at Airbnbs, chances are you have some stories that you can't wait to tell the world. Stories about connection. Trust. Unlikely friendships with people you never expected to meet, but who have become an important part of your life.

Share your stories! People are hungry to hear more about the 99.99 percent of humans who are essentially good, just as you are.

I can't wait to read your stories.

Photo by Studio414.com

About the Author

TRUDY OHNSORG HAS TRAVELED TO MANY PARTS OF THE WORLD, BEGINNING WHEN SHE BOUGHT A ONE-WAY TICKET TO JAPAN AFTER COLLEGE. She discovered Airbnb during a month in Costa Rica in 2012 and became an Airbnb host herself in 2015. According to Trudy, hosting changed her life:

> "Sharing your home is not just transactional - it can be transformational. You learn radical trust when you welcome strangers into your home and life."

Trudy's career has balanced a focus on health policy (she was Minnesota's Director for Interagency Health Reform) with a love of nature and creativity (she was an award-winning landscape designer who taught a senior-level landscape design course for a dozen years). Currently, Trudy is a partner in a consulting group that provides strategic guidance for nonprofits. Trudy lives in a little purple house in Saint Paul, Minnesota.

For information, contact: Trudy Ohnsorg, c/o Bohemian Treehouse Press, LLC
    1125 Burns Avenue, Saint Paul, MN 55106
    www.AirBeNMe.com, info@AirBeNMe.com
    Facebook, Twitter, Instagram: AirBeNMe
    Podcast: Air Be & Being